COPYWRITING FOR THE ENTREPRENEUR

HOW TO WRITE 10,000 WORDS IN 2-3 HOURS

A.J. CRAFT

Copywriting for the Entrepreneur:
How to Write 10,000 Words in 2-3 Hours
By A.J. Craft

CreateSpace Edition
Copyright © 2017 by A.J. Craft

Cover designed by: A. J. Craft
Published by: A. J. Craft at CreateSpace

Letter From the Author

Thank you for purchasing my book. I hope you find the information useful. Remember that information is only as effective as your decision to take massive action, so nothing in this book will work unless you put it into practice consistently.

If you would like more information about my copywriting courses, would like to work with me, or receive free tips, tricks and techniques, visit my website at www.craftywriter.com.

Thank you again for your patronage, now let's get to writing!

-A.J. Craft

Introduction

Do you hate writing? Would you rather have all your teeth pulled out without anesthesia using medieval tools while the dental assistant pours lemon juice down your throat? Is that how much you hate writing?

Or perhaps you don't necessarily hate it, you just realize that every time you sit down to write something, it's also about time you cleaned out the scummy residue from all those plumbing pipes around the house. And compared to writing, you actually look forward to that more.

If either one of those scenarios sounds like you, then you're gonna love this book. It's for the procrastinator.

It's for the English class dropout.

It's for those of us who can't quite make the connection between brain to keyboard.

If that's you, then you need this book.

Writing content doesn't have to be boring, painful, or take a ton of time. In fact, it can be, dare I say-fun? That's not a typo. When you have an organized system in place and you know exactly what you're about to sit down and write, it empowers you to know that you can do this and do it well.

Not only that, but you're going to find that you'll be able to pump out content so much faster than you've ever been able to before. And that means more time for you to focus on other things in your business.

But funny things can happen to you. You're going to notice that there will be a spike in audience interest. All those Facebook posts are going to get a lot more "likes" and comments than you're used to. Those blog posts on your website are also going to show an increase in readership and comments.

And instead of your email list unsubscribing, they're going to save all your emails in a special folder to read over and over again because you've given them so much good information and ideas. They're going to realize that you are a very valuable resource for them to have.

Know what happens after that? You become a subject-matter expert in your field. People start coming you for advice-and for your products and services.

And before you know it, you're nose-deep in clients and cash.

But it all starts with writing great content that gives your target audience useful information so they can apply it to their own business and lives. You have to develop a relationship with them so they come to know, like, and trust you. Only then can you serve them by selling.

But here's the thing.

In order for this book to work for you, and in order for you to see fast results, you're going to need to keep an open mind. What I mean by that is, you're going to have to be willing to try something new.

The reason I'm addressing this is because a lot of people will purchase a program or course, not really commit to it, or go through it to the end, only to turn around and halfheartedly try to implement it. When it doesn't work, they tell the world that it's a scam.

This formula is nothing like that. I personally use it every single day to write anywhere between 5,000 and 10,000 words. If I didn't want to do silly human things like take breaks and live my life, I could probably get in 30,000 words a day with this formula.

But the point isn't necessarily how many words you can cram into a 24-hour period of time. It's about being able to have a strategy to create enough content to fill up an entire week's worth of social media and website posts in a matter of hours.

It's about getting you comfortable with writing so that it no longer feels like a horrible chore that you have to do for something that you assume you can't do. I'm here to tell you that you can do it. Not only that, you can do it well. You just have to be willing to put in the work.

The best part about this is that I'm over dramatizing it. There really isn't a lot to the formula itself. Except of course, for learning it. But once you learn how to organize content and how to come up with your content ideas, then it will fly by and it will become second nature to you.

It's only in the beginning that it will take a little learning curve, so know that going into it and don't give up. It WILL work for you if you're willing to work it.

So enough with that. let's get started.

This is Why You Hate Writing Content

I understand why you might dislike creating content. Especially if you don't particularly enjoy writing content in the first place. It can be hard when you don't know what to say. Staring at a blank piece of paper or a flashing cursor does very little to help you.

Maybe you do know what to say and you ramble on and on because your message is unclear and you're not sure how to make it more clear. That leads to frustration and an urge to quit which reinforces your desire to procrastinate.

Another reason why you may hate writing content is because, other than the fact that you know you're supposed to create it, you don't really know why you're doing it. Yes, you know that content is king. That's what they say, but it doesn't really resonate with you. You'd rather just throw up a bunch of filler content, cross your fingers and hope that does the trick. It doesn't work that way.

Sometimes it gets confusing to create content. You get lost in all the different tips, techniques, and tricks that you can talk about an end up muddling them all together where there is no central point or theme. This can cause your audience to struggle to read your copy and confused about what you're trying to say.

When you do write content and slap it up on your blog or your social media posts, you rarely, if ever get a response from your audience. They're just not plugged in to what you're saying. Feeling rejected can do a lot to keep you from consistently creating content.

Maybe you hate it at all, but you just don't know how to write. You were never good in English class and you never had a desire to continue your writing after school. Maybe you do appreciate the value of providing content, but you don't know how to write and you don't have the money to pay somebody to do it for you.

These are all valid reasons why you feel the way you do about copy. I'm here to tell you that writing copy is the number one concern that should be on your mind. If you are in business for yourself, it is the absolute lifeblood connecting you and dollar bills together.

If you don't know how to communicate with your audience and deliver precise messages that hit them emotionally, you'll never sell anything.

I get so frustrated sometimes when I see business owners spending time on busy work projects trying to perfect their website, or their business cards, or doing everything else that they could possibly do to spin their wheels other than writing content that reaches their audience and converts them into customers.

Don't let this be you. If it is you, then stop it immediately. Obviously if you're reading this book, then you know that you need to do something different. You know that you need to get better at writing copy and you're looking for the how. The great news is that I'm going to show you some techniques on how I write copy and then I'm going to show you how to do it so quickly that it no longer becomes painful. In fact, dare I say it might even be fun.

But the first thing that you need to do before you read any further is change your mindset. You need to understand that in order to pour this information you're about to read in your brain, you need to let go of old belief systems and patterns that you've been doing in your life.

In other words, the negative self talk about not being able to write or not wanting to write has to go. You have to change your mindset and your attitude to welcome learning how to do it and repeating to yourself that you love doing it.

Your mind follows your body and when you can control your mind to focus on the things you need to get done, the body will follow.

It's all about the copy when it comes to selling anything and it's all about the copy when it comes to helping other people.

There's no way around it. There's no busy work that can replace it. Yes, the systems can be learned quickly and can be learned by anybody, but the action is what brings it into reality.

Are you ready to take action?

What You'll Learn in this Book

Connect with your audience.
From the first paragraph of your copy, you need to connect with your audience on a personal level, reaching into their hearts, and appeal to their emotional side as you speak to them. They have to know that you get them. And once you have their attention, and show them how much you care, then you can sell them.

Use your personal experiences as material for an unlimited number of article ideas. Your audience wants YOU. That's who they're buying. Not your products or services, they want you. They like who you are, what you represent, and just need a reason to follow you.

You're going to learn how to give them that reason.

Overcome objections before you ever share your offer. Contrary to what most of us do, writing isn't about sitting down and writing what comes out of your head and making it perfect the first time. There needs to be a certain amount organization that takes place first so that your thoughts and ideas transfer in the right order. You're going to learn how to handle objections before they even object.

Ask for the sale without selling. How do you do that? I promise there's a very special technique that increases sales by doing it this way. The best part? Your audience doesn't mind it.

Simultaneously give them help full tips and sell your products and services. You don't have to worry about whether you're giving all your good information away for free. There is no such thing.

Write more in less time. A lot more. A ton more. Did I mention that you're going to write more in less time?

Avoid writer's block, anxiety, and procrastination. Once you learn the formula, the subject of writing copy will no longer make you cringe. You're going to love the fact that you're able to do it quickly and give high-quality content to your audience.

Write 500-1,000-word articles and blog posts in minutes. You read that correctly. You will literally be able to write an entire email, blog post, or article in just a few minutes.

Structure your content to keep your audience's interest all the way to the end. It's not just about the amount of words on the page, it's about creating useful content. And that's exactly what you're going to learn how to do to keep them reading and coming back for more.

But First...Do You Know Who Your Target Audience is?

The secret to creating content that emotionally captures your audience's attention, plays with their hearts, and compels them to do what you are selling is this: knowing your target audience.

Do you know what that means? Are you sure? Because most people don't really know their target audience. They start a business around a product or service they assume will sell because it sounds like a good idea, without ever doing any kind of market research or getting to know what kind of customers they want to target. As a result, they usually fail.

You actually need to reverse that and do it in the opposite order. Understanding who is going to buy your products is critical if you want to sell to them.

Most business owners assume that a target audience consists of basic demographics, including age, gender, and occupation. Let me ask you this, let's say you were to pick a random stranger off the street and tell him your name, age, and what you do for living. Would that stranger be able to tell you your deepest struggles and fears just by the information you gave him? Would he be able to tell you what keeps you up at night? What makes you deliriously happy? What you're dreams and ambitions are, or what you want for your kids?

Obviously not, so why would any of us think that we could sell a product or service to an audience only knowing that same limited information? Look, I get it. It sounds like a bunch of trouble and hassle to take the time to research. I promise you that if you do the legwork on the front end, you can use that information for every single piece of content that you write. You can use that information for every single decision you make in your business. And nine times out of 10, you're going to be spot on.

Why do you think that companies spend millions of dollars conducting market research and surveys? Surely they have better things to do with their money if it didn't matter, right?

You don't have to be a large corporation with millions of dollars in the bank in order to conduct your own survey and research about customer practices. But you have to be willing to do it in the first place.

I want to encourage you that before you put the practices in this book to work, discover who your target audience is. I have a book that goes along with this series that teaches you how to find your tribe and market to your target audience. You can find it where you purchased this book.

One of the most important things you can learn is how to find your exact target audience. This is sometimes called your customer avatar. It's the detailed questions that you ask yourself about how this group of people specifically lives.

A great way to formulate questions in order to use them to find the answers is to start with yourself. Ask yourself what do you like to do in your spare time? What are your hobbies and interests? What kind of toothpaste to you use and why? And yes, you really do need to be this specific.

Somebody who works will have different priorities than somebody who sits on the couch all day. Somebody who goes to church faithfully every single week will have different value systems than somebody who never attends church.

My advice would be to keep a running list of these questions so that you have it as a template every time you're trying to identify a new target audience. If you have a business that targets multiple audiences, then you want to do a separate research panel for each target audience.

Again, this is priceless information for your business, and it's something that once you've done, you'll be able to use over and over again. Not to mention the fact that it's going to speed up creating content and copy and it will solidify in your mind exactly who you're talking to.

Please do not ignore my advice. Find out your target audience before you do anything else.

The Difference Between Content and Money-Making Content

Now that you know exactly who your target audience is, (because you've taken the time to research and figure it out), you can start thinking about what kind of content you want to give them.

There's an important distinction that I want to make to you. There is a difference between creating content and creating money-making content. And what I mean is this, you can summarize a previous article that tells you how to do something. You can make it your own and give the information a spin before publishing it. That's fine, but it's most likely considered filler content.

Filler content can be helpful to give quick tips and tricks when you need to create something quickly, but most of the time it's a waste of your time. That's because every single time you create content you should create it in the exact system that I'm going to teach you in the next few chapters.

Why?

Because you want to maximize every single opportunity you have to connect with your audience by combining two things.

First, you want to give them valuable information that they can take and use in their business almost immediately. Second, then you want to format a call to action at the bottom of every single piece of content.

You want the reader to be conditioned to know that when they come on your page, or read your post, they'll be asked to do something.

This can vary from asking about your product or signing up for your email subscription newsletter, or whatever. But you must ask them to do something.

When you learn how to write money-making content you increase your sales. You never know until you ask, right? So if you never ask, then how do you know? Get into the habit of requiring yourself to put a call to action at the bottom of every post.

Again, that doesn't mean you have to sell something every single time. What it means is that you can get creative. Maybe you want them to sign up for giveaway where you're giving something free away to a lucky winner. Or you're running some kind of contest that you know they can benefit from. You can be creative, but you need to be consistent over everything else.

The Content Formula

The formula that I'm about to teach you is priceless. It can absolutely propel you into writing tons of content in a very short time. However, there are some things I want you to know before you go on.

First, it will not work if you don't work it. That means if you doubt yourself or tell yourself it won't work, most likely it isn't going to work. You have to have the right mindset and the willingness to be open enough to try it and try it several times. The more you get into the habit of doing, the faster you will become.

It doesn't take very long at all to create high quality content quickly. In fact, you can absolutely create a week's worth of content in about an hour implementing it the first couple times. But if you look at it like it's too much trouble or too much organized chaos and you don't take the time to learn it, this book is useless to you.

Second, it will take some time to outline and edit, but not a lot of time. The point is to get out the information that's in your head on the page as quickly as possible. How can a sculptor sculpt a masterpiece if he has no clay to work with?

One of the biggest writing myths that for some reason continues to be perpetuated is that writing means putting down words perfectly the first time. That's not true, nor has it ever been true. Writing is a process. That includes beginning with an outline. The outline IS part of the writing. So it does count. And you can count that as part of your word count or daily goals.

So it will take a very short amount of time to outline before you fill in the rest of the copy. Then you'll go back and you'll edit it. So writing a week's worth of content in about an hour will be the process of outlining and then filling in the rest of the content. I'll explain this in more detail as we go along.

Step 1: Identify your topic

Before you do anything, you have to know exactly what you want to write about. That means you need to understand what message you want to deliver. You should already know who your target audience is and what their needs are, so delivering the message is going to come a lot easier to you now.

In fact, through the process of finding your target audience, you will discover that there are several problems they need solved. All you have to do is make a list of these problems. Now each one of these problems becomes a topic for a post or article. That's another great reason for advocating finding out your target market (just saying).

The next step will be to decide on how many words your article or blog post will be. Usually, 500 words is sufficient to keep your readers' interest and short enough that they can get through the article, but not too long they click off your site. But whatever type of content you're writing, determine how many words you want it to be.

Then, double check that the topics you are covering center around your business and position your business as the solution to their problems. You want to give them useful content, but the content must be narrowly defined to something you can help them with later.

Every piece of content should give tons of value and helpful information to your audience about a specific problem they are having trouble with. Not only is this going to help them, but it's also going to establish you as the expert who they may need to return to again and again to solve their other problems.

Remember, always focus on service before selling. You can't sell them anything until they know that you care about helping them first. Not to mention this makes selling a breeze and almost no effort, but you have to have a sincere and caring heart to want to help them order won't work. People can spot a sleazy salesman further away than a shark can smell blood in the water.

There are several ways that you can brainstorm and many techniques to help you do it. Mind mapping is just one of those ways and it's a great way to relate several topics to a central idea. What's so important about using a tool to help you brainstorm is that you get all of your ideas out of your head and onto paper.

A lot of us believe that we can keep our ideas swirling around in our head indefinitely, but most of the time that's not true. Instead, ideas float out of our mind as quickly as they came in, and we've lost the opportunity to capture and document them.

Using a mind map process allows you to visually see on paper what you're looking at and more accurately assess the best direction you want to take.

Another thing you can do is to go into Facebook groups and see what problems, complaints, and struggles people are talking about. This is a phenomenal way to find research information and a very quick and easy way. All you have to do is create a swipe file and put all of the ideas and information into one place and refer to it at a later time. From here, you will have endless ideas about content and they'll all be right on point because they're already going to solve a problem that your customers have.

Don't worry about giving away too much free information-there is no such thing! It's a natural tendency to believe that we need to save our best premium packages and products. To give it away for free sounds crazy, right?

Actually, the opposite is true. You should give away your best premium stuff up front to your prospects. That's because it establishes you as an expert who knows what they're talking about. They still need your services and products because only you can teach them, or deliver in a way that they can understand.

So, let's recap:

•You have to know what you want to write about before you start. (This is based on knowing your target audience and their needs.)

•Decide on how many words your article or blog post will be.

•Ideally, the topics you cover will center around your business.

•But they should PRIMARILY give tons of value and helpful information to your target audience.

•Service BEFORE selling.

•Mind mapping is a good way to relate several topics to a central idea.

•The best way is to go into Facebook groups and see what problems, complaints, and struggles people are talking about and then create a list of articles explaining how to solve their problems.

•Don't worry about giving away too much free information- there is no such thing!

•Your goal should be to give away dump truck loads of quality advice and tips so that your audience sees you as the subject-matter "go-to" professional.

•THAT'S how you get a steady flow of clients.

•More content + more often =more clients.

•Brainstorm as many topic ideas that relate to your business from the perspective of "how can I help my audience today?"

Step 2: The 5 Sections

There are 5 sections of your article that should be structured in a way that:

-Captures the reader's attention

-Emotionally draws them in

-Explains the purpose of the article and gives helpful information

-Handles any objections

-Solves their problem in some way

-Presents some form of call-to-action or required action from the reader

We're going to go over each section right now.

Section 1: The "Me Too" Connection

Introductory paragraph must hook your audience. The entire effectiveness of your message begins and ends here. If your first paragraph doesn't grab their attention, make them stop and look at what you have to say, you might as well not even write your article or blog post. They're going to click off and go on to something else. You only have about three seconds to grab their attention.

The best way to do that is to tell a story or share a personal experience. People love stories and people have been telling stories for thousands of years. It's still the leading technique for getting a person's attention. If you can make them compelling, intriguing, and even shocking, you will hold their focus until the end of your message.

However, don't use too many "I's." People want to know what's in it for them and they don't care about your experience as much as they care about their own. Make sure that you use as few first-person words as possible when you can.

 Ask questions. Even if the rhetorical questions. It makes the reader stop and ask themselves if they can relate to you or your story. This also creates interest for them to keep reading.

The goal in creating your content is to get them to think "me too" in their head instead of saying "so what?" You want them to be able to identify with your experience in the story, so write it in the way that makes it easy for them to do that.

Example:

•Boring:

"I knew at age twelve that I was going to help people. I had an ability to show others how to better themselves and ever since then I've been following my passion to help women achieve their dreams."

*(Notice how many "**I's**" there are?)*

•More interesting:

"When my best friend told me she wanted to kill herself at age 12, and I convinced her to wait to see one more sunrise so that enough time was bought to get her some help, I knew my purpose on this floating blue-green orb was to change lives.

*Have you ever experienced a traumatic
turning point like that in your own life?"*

Quick Recap:

•Introductory paragraph MUST hook
your audience.

•If it doesn't, they will leave.

•Best way to do that is to tell a story or
share a personal experience. (The more
shocking, gripping, amazing, the better)

•BUT don't use too many "I's." (It's a
killer)

•Instead, ask questions or tell a story.

•Your goal is to get them to think "me
too" in their heads instead of "so what?"

Section 2: How it Works

These are the logistics of your topic, idea, tips, and techniques. Often called features. This is where you can explain to them how it works.

However, you are going to speak technically to them. Instead, you're going to explain the benefits of having this product or service, and how all helped their lives.

Try to sell whenever you not positioning your message in such a way that they're open to accepting it.

Example:

"The process of healing yoga can be simplified in six steps..."

Section 3: Object to the Objections

Many times in sales you get to the end of your sales pitch and find out that you haven't answered all of the objections that the customers a throw out to you.

It's no different when you're writing content. People are naturally skeptical, so they're not going to believe you initially until you offer them reasons why they should.

That's why you need to handle objections on the front end before they have a chance to formulate their own their own questions and basically object.

Sometimes in copy, people will handle this by writing a section of frequently asked questions. That is one way of doing it, but another way would be to handle the objections as you're writing the content.

So throughout the page, you will address objections that will answer the questions in their head. The trick is to be able to anticipate what those objections are.

It's pretty easy to do, because most of them are common questions that almost anybody would ask.

When you address their objections upfront, you set your solution up to be more readily accepted. That means you're building trust because they feel like you know who they are and how to help them with their problem.

When you can tell somebody that you've been there too, and that you had the same doubts as they have, and then explain to them how you handled it, you draw them into trusting you more.

This is also the place where you're going to describe the pain they will experience if they don't take action right away.

This is extremely important because if you don't show them why they need your service or product they won't be compelled to buy it when it comes time for you to ask for the sale.

You can use a variety of literary tools such as imagery, metaphor, or paint a picture in your audience's mind. But what you want to do is make it explicit and very grim.

You need to describe the pain in the most horrific terms so that they really feel how bad it's going to be if they don't solve the problem immediately.

Some people feel like this is manipulation. That is technically correct, and all of us- every single one of us- manipulate people every single day.

Let me explain.

The word manipulation has had a negative connotation attached to it, but really it is the act of persuading someone in one direction or another.

Every time your children beg and plead and scream and cry to get you to buy that sugary cereal they want until you give in is a form of manipulation.

As long as you're not using your skills to do them harm or to only serve yourself, you should never feel guilty about trying to persuade somebody. Especially if you know that what you have to offer is in their best interest and will make their lives 1000% better.

It is your job. It is your duty to persuade them to take action on something that will help them in their lives.

Example:

•*"So, you're thinking that healing yoga is just a bunch of hyped up hippie magic, right? Let me show you how a 95-year old retired school teacher spends her days showing kindergarteners how to do cartwheels…"*

•*"At first, I thought ten grand was a lot of money too. Until I realized that I had spent three times that amount doing everything myself, and I was still in the same place I started..."*

Quick Recap:

•You will discuss all the objections that the reader might be thinking.

•By addressing them first, you set your solution up to be more readily accepted.

•Also, you will describe the pain they will experience if they don't do it.

•Use imagery, metaphor, paint a picture in the audience's mind; make it grim, unbearable.

•Your job is to help them, so make them realize how awful life will be without your product or service.

Section 4: Solve their Problem

You are about to brighten their world because you can show them something that's going to alleviate their pain and solve their problem.

It's critically important that you convey that message in a clear and descriptive way. You want to explain to them in great detail how their life will improve once they take your advice and incorporate your solution into their lives.

Failing to do this is a huge disservice to your customers because without your solution you're going to keep them in their current pain. So it's up to you to do a good job explaining how you can help them leave their pain behind.

Paint them a wonderful picture of how they will feel after they have taken your solution and applied it to their lives. Make it as emotionally compelling as possible and don't leave out any part that will show them how every aspect of their life will improve.

Be sure to explain the "how-to" or features, of your solution by describing the benefits and how it will help them when they use it. This is important. You want to appeal to their emotional side, not their logical side. Features are a logical list of facts while benefits are an emotional picture of how their pain will be alleviated by accepting it.

Example:

•*"How incredible would it be to roll out of bed in the morning without one creaking joint or aching body part? Running around all day with energy to spare when you get home?"*

•*"Can you imagine how investing in yourself can change your entire family's life? And not only your immediate family, but future generations as well?"*

Quick recap:

•Let them know how their life will improve once they take your advice/incorporate your helpful information into their lives/buy your product or service.

•Paint them a pretty picture; make it as emotionally compelling as possible and don't leave out any part that will show them how every aspect of their life will improve.

•Explain how the "how to" or features of your solution will benefit them when they apply it.

Section 5: Ask for the Call to Action

This is very important. Even when you're doing an informational article or blog post, where the sole purpose is to benefit the reader, you must include a call to action. Always.

You want to condition the reader to understand that when they hear from you. You are always going to condition them to do something. Whether that's something for themselves or something in the direction of their own lives. You always want them to do something.

Never end any piece of content without asking or requiring your audience to take some form of action. A call to action can be more than just selling. It can be asking for the sale, inserting a link to your website and telling them to go to it, offering a free e-book or other piece of content, and/or opting into your email list, that sort of thing.

Example:

•*"Stop letting yourself down and demand that you take action right now. Click here.."*

•*"Want to learn how you can use every single one of these tips to make more money? Download this free guide.."*

•*"Get weekly tips that will keep you accountable, yield terrific results and ensure that you are moving toward your goal. Sign up here…"*

Quick recap:

•Always, Always, ALWAYS include some type of call-to-action in your content.

•NEVER, NEVER, NEVER end any piece of content without asking or requiring your audience to take some form of action.

•This can include:

-Asking for the sale

-Inserting a link to your website

-Offering a free Ebook or other piece of content

-Opting in to your email list

Step 3: Divide Each Section

So up until now we've learned how to determine what's going to get your reader's attention. You're going to get your audience's attention, hook them, bring them in and paint the terrible picture of what they're going to miss out on and how their life will be worse if they don't take the solution. Then you're going to paint the picture of how great it will be If they do take the solution. And then you can add the call to action.

This leads us to Step 3.

This is where you will divide each section into equal parts based on word count. (Example: For a 500-word article, each section will have 100 words)

Within each section, each main idea or tip will list an equal number of bullet points (if each section is 100 words, then there will be four bullet points, 25 words each)

Divide Each Section Example:

Section 1: Hook, attention-grabber, story time "me too" connection (100 words)

Section 2: How the solution works (100 words)

Section 3: Object to the objections (The pain of not doing it) (100 words)

Section 4: The solution (The pleasure if they do it) (100 words)

Section 5: Call to Action (Tell them exactly what you want them to do) (100 words)

Section 1: Hook, attention-grabber, story time "me too" connection (100 words)

  -Topic 1 (25 words)

  -Topic 2 (25 words)

  -Topic 3 (25 words)

  -Topic 4 (25 words)

Section 2: How the solution works (100 words)

  -Topic 1 (25 words)

  -Topic 2 (25 words)

  -Topic 3 (25 words)

  -Topic 4 (25 words)

Section 3: Object to the objections (The pain of not doing it) (100 words)

-Topic 1 (25 words)

  -Topic 2 (25 words)

-Topic 3 (25 words)

-Topic 4 (25 words)

Section 4: The solution (The pleasure if they do it) (100 words)

-Topic 1 (25 words)

-Topic 2 (25 words)

-Topic 3 (25 words)

-Topic 4 (25 words)

Section 5: Call to Action (Tell them exactly what you want them to do) (100 words)

-Topic 1 (25 words)

-Topic 2 (25 words)

-Topic 3 (25 words)

-Topic 4 (25 words)

Quick Recap:

•Divide each section into equal parts based on word count. (Example: For a 500-word article, each section will have 100 words)
•Within each section, each main idea or tip will list an equal number of bullet points (If each section is 100 words, then there will be 4 bullet points, 25 words each)

Step 4: Add the Details

Add 2-3 sentences about the details of your main topic and how it relates to them.
When possible, comment on your personal experience with the topic.

If you can put that "me too" thought in their head, it's great because it builds rapport and trust with them. So, for example, in topic one you have three sentences, and each one of those sentences is broken down into details.

Section 1: Hook, attention-grabber, story time "me too" connection (100 words)

   -Topic 1 (25 words)

*Sentence 1: Detail about the topic and how it relates to your audience.

*Sentence 2: Detail about the topic and how it relates to your audience.

*Sentence 3: Detail about the topic and how it relates to your audience.

Quick Recap:

- Add 2-3 sentences about the details of your main topic and how it relates to them.
- When possible, comment on your personal experience with the topic.

This formula alone will dramatically speed up your writing time

It may not feel like it because it's an outline and you have to mentally and purposely plan it out. But how much time are you wasting by procrastinating and not doing anything at all because you have this jumble of messages in your head and feelings or sentiments that you want to get on paper, but you don't know in what order or how? So you're actually taking action by doing it this way in a planned and organized way.

The Secret Weapon

This is what has me writing 5,000 to 10,000 words in a day within 2 to 3 hours. Yes, seriously. I maintain this word count daily when I do my own writing or ghostwrite for other clients in both fiction and non-fiction.

There's one secret that will speed up this entire process even faster. It will allow you to write so fast that you can prepare a week's worth of content in about an hour, or a month's worth of content in one day. It's the key to writing and releasing content at lightning speed. And that is….

Speech-to-text software

This outline formula you just learned will already speed up your content writing, but if you want to write even faster, then you need some kind of speech-to-text software.

There are a couple of different systems to choose from but I use Dragon Naturally Speaking (The Premium version). It will transcribe as you speak with surprising accuracy. And one of the great things about it is that as you use it, it learns and improves with you.

So, let's say you're going to the beach or to the park or you're going to travel. You can record your voice and transcribe your notes later. If you have a hard time shutting your business off in your head and you're used to making mental notes and then forgetting them because you have no way of writing them down, or if you're supposed to be out with family, but you can't get your ideas out of your head until you write them down, then a quick message on your phone can record those ideas to transcribe later. It's better than other speech-to-text software programs in my opinion.

BUT there's another way that you can use it to write content from anywhere at anytime without a computer. There is a feature in the premium version that allows you to download your digital recordings. So if you use your phone or a handheld voice recorder, you can take it anywhere with you and transcribe content later. It is my best secret weapon to create a ton of content fast!

Step 5: Editing

This is not exactly the most fun part of writing, but it is necessary.

Don't edit immediately after writing your content. Go on to the next article and let some time pass before coming back to it. It doesn't have to be a long period of time. If you're on a deadline and you're trying to get this out, it can be five or ten minutes, that sort of thing. But your brain does need a rest from looking at it so that it can gain a little bit of perspective.

Use short sentences (easier for the reader to scan and still get the main ideas). But it's more than that. Shorter sentences also make a rhythmic point. It helps reflect the way that you talk to people in person. It draws their eye downward very quickly.

They can get through the article quickly and get the message of what you're trying to say. That actually catches their attention. So when you're making it so easy for them to read and you're putting your message in short sentences, it will actually get them to slow down and re-read to internalize your message and read it carefully. It's like another attention grabber.

Go through your article, pick out every commonly used verb and use a Thesaurus to replace it with a more vivid, colorful verb. Verbs are a writer's dream because they really do the work for painting that picture and setting the mood, tone and energy. This sounds like it would take a long time, but you can go to Thesaurus.com and type in the word that you're using and it will give you a list of synonyms.

What will happen is the more you practice, the more you automatically know how to draw from the words you've used before. Your mind will point out the verbs when you're trying to use a common verb and prompt you to use something more comfortable.

Find opportunities to insert a metaphor or imagery whenever you can. A metaphor can be a vivid way to relate something that everybody knows, a reference point that everybody can understand and to your message.

Use Grammarly to check spelling and grammar. They have a Chrome extension that is handy and free. Once you upload it, it will check everything you're working on for grammar and spelling. For example, if you're on Facebook or open a Word document, it will point out incorrectly spelled words by putting a red line underneath them, and you can click on that and it'll give you a list of alternative words and help you fix them. It's pretty great.

Double and triple check for any spelling errors. Make sure that you know the basics like you're and your, their, there and they're and when to use those and in which way.

Everybody gets up in arms when they see a misspelled word. I'm guilty of the same thing. I'm a writer and I'm guilty of judging other people for not catching their mistakes. But I'm also guilty of not catching my own, either. It happens.

A person can be a genius and if they misspell a word or use the wrong form of it by accident, we start questioning their education and background. Just remember that done is better than perfect. So you want to do the best you can with spelling and grammar errors. If someone points it out, correct it, and move on and don't beat yourself up about it.

Read it out loud to ensure it makes sense. Make sure it makes sense. Sometimes we think in our head our words are brilliant, but actually sound awkward and weird when we say it out loud. Reading your writing out loud will also reaffirm whether your writing reflects the way we talk to people in person or not.

Insert any and all necessary links before posting. It's easy to forget that. I always like to highlight where the links go in red. It stands out to me and I can insert them as one of the last things to do before I hit publish.

Massive Action Exercise

1.Brainstorm a list of blog topic ideas that are problem areas for your target audience. Then, next to each problem, list the solution.

2.Now outline each blog post (just outline, don't start writing yet). When finished, go onto the next article and do that until you have at least five.

3.Then go back to the first article and complete the next step in the formula. The idea is to essentially write 5 articles at the same time, finishing the same step in each article before moving on to the next step. This interrupts your brain so that it has a fresh perspective for each article every time you look at it.

Repeat this process every time you sit down to write and you will have written a week's worth of content in about an hour. It really does work, but you have to be committed to following the formula.

Final Thoughts

I hope that this book has provided some insight and will help you write faster content. Can you see how you can completely revolutionize your time management system and create content fast?

Actually, it starts to become fun, trust me. As I said before, you have to implement this for it to work. Get started immediately by creating your brainstorming list and then follow this formula and see how fast it happens.

Even if you're not using speech-to-text software and you're just doing the outlined steps, it's going to completely revolutionize the time in which you get this done.

I'm very excited to give you this information and would love to hear

about your progress. You can contact
me at: **www.CraftyWriter.com**

Also, if you'd like to hire me to write for
you, or to take one of my several
copywriting courses, head over to my
website and send me a message.

All my best to you and your crafty writing
adventures!

-A.J.